About the author

Somdip Dey, FRSA

Somdip Dey, FRSA, also professionally known as InteliDey, is an Embedded Artificial Intelligence scientist, engineer, entrepreneur, AI art & music creator and TED speaker. Dey is the CEO of Nosh Technologies, the CTO of Blockway Technologies and a Lecturer at the University of Essex, UK. He is also the Danah Zohar Professor of Quantum Philosophy & Professor of Practice (AI/ML) at Woxsen University, India. He has more than 13 years of industrial experience including working for Microsoft and Samsung in developing numerous technological products that are currently used by billions of people in different ways. For contributions to improving society through applications of embedded machine learning Dey is elected a Life Fellow of the Royal Society of Arts, named an MIT Innovator Under 35, an Outstanding Achiever in Education,

Science & Innovation at the 2023 India UK Achievers Honours and a 2022 World IP Review Leader. He is also a member of the Forbes Technology Council and regularly appears in news including Forbes, Entrepreneur, Business Insider, Tech Crunch and many more.

Table of Contents

CHAPTER 1: EMBRACING THE FRUGAL MINDSET: THE LEAN ENTREPRENEUR'S PHILOSOPHY 7

    INTRODUCTION 7
    THE LEAN ENTREPRENEUR'S PHILOSOPHY 7
    HOW TO DEVELOP A FRUGAL MINDSET 9
    FRUGAL MINDSET IN ACTION: REAL-LIFE EXAMPLES 11
    CONCLUSION 12

CHAPTER 2: THE ART OF BOOTSTRAPPING: FUNDING YOUR STARTUP WITH LIMITED RESOURCES 13

    INTRODUCTION 13
    THE POWER OF BOOTSTRAPPING 13
    BOOTSTRAPPING STRATEGIES FOR SUCCESS 14
    CONCLUSION 16

CHAPTER 3: BUILDING A LEAN TEAM: HIRING AND RETAINING TOP TALENT ON A BUDGET 18

    INTRODUCTION 18
    THE IMPORTANCE OF A LEAN TEAM 18
    STRATEGIES FOR BUILDING A LEAN TEAM 19
    RETAINING TOP TALENT ON A BUDGET 21
    CONCLUSION 22

CHAPTER 4: MAXIMIZING MINIMUM VIABLE PRODUCTS: TESTING AND VALIDATING IDEAS WITH LESS 23

    INTRODUCTION 23
    THE POWER OF MINIMUM VIABLE PRODUCTS 23
    MAXIMIZING YOUR MINIMUM VIABLE PRODUCT 24
    CONCLUSION 26

CHAPTER 5: AGILE MARKETING: PROMOTING YOUR STARTUP WITHOUT BREAKING THE BANK 28

    INTRODUCTION 28
    UNDERSTANDING AGILE MARKETING 28
    AGILE MARKETING STRATEGIES FOR LEAN ENTREPRENEURS 29
    PRACTICAL TIPS FOR PROMOTING YOUR STARTUP ON A BUDGET ... 30
    CONCLUSION 32

CHAPTER 6: COST-EFFECTIVE CUSTOMER ACQUISITION: ATTRACTING AND RETAINING CLIENTS THE LEAN WAY 34

- INTRODUCTION 34
- COST-EFFECTIVE CUSTOMER ACQUISITION STRATEGIES...............................34
- RETAINING CLIENTS THE LEAN WAY 35
- CONCLUSION 37

CHAPTER 7: STREAMLINING OPERATIONS: HOW TO ELIMINATE WASTE AND BOOST EFFICIENCY 39

- INTRODUCTION 39
- IDENTIFYING WASTE IN YOUR OPERATIONS 39
- STRATEGIES FOR STREAMLINING OPERATIONS 40
- BOOSTING EFFICIENCY THROUGH LEAN PRINCIPLES 42
- CONCLUSION 43

CHAPTER 8: SCALING SMART: GROWING YOUR BUSINESS WITH LEAN PRINCIPLES...44

- INTRODUCTION 44
- KEY FACTORS FOR SMART SCALING 44
- STRATEGIES FOR SCALING WITH LEAN PRINCIPLES 45
- CONCLUSION 47

CHAPTER 9: PARTNERSHIPS AND COLLABORATIONS: LEVERAGING NETWORKS FOR MUTUAL SUCCESS 49

- INTRODUCTION 49
- THE BENEFITS OF PARTNERSHIPS AND COLLABORATIONS..............................49
- STRATEGIES FOR BUILDING SUCCESSFUL PARTNERSHIPS AND COLLABORATIONS 50
- TIPS FOR NURTURING AND MAINTAINING PARTNERSHIPS.............................51
- CONCLUSION 52

CHAPTER 10: THE FRUGAL FOUNDER'S TOOLKIT: ESSENTIAL RESOURCES AND STRATEGIES FOR LEAN ENTREPRENEURSHIP.........54

- INTRODUCTION 54
- PRODUCTIVITY AND ORGANIZATION TOOLS 54
- MARKETING RESOURCES..55
- FINANCIAL MANAGEMENT 55
- TIME MANAGEMENT AND SELF-CARE..56
- CONCLUSION 56

BONUS CHAPTER: GETTING FEATURED IN NEWS BY JOURNALISTS AND CONTRIBUTORS...58

Introduction 58
Why Getting Featured in News Matters 58
Strategies for Getting Featured in News 59
Maximizing the Impact of Your Media Coverage 60
Conclusion 61

BONUS CHAPTER: HOW TO FIND THE RIGHT CO-FOUNDER 63

Introduction 63
The Importance of a Co-founder 63
Finding the Right Co-founder 64
Formalizing the Co-founder Relationship 65
Conclusion 66

BONUS CHAPTER: SHOULD I BOTHER PARTICIPATING IN A STARTUP ACCELERATOR? 68

Introduction 68
Understanding Startup Accelerators 68
The Pros of Joining a Startup Accelerator 69
The Cons of Joining a Startup Accelerator 70
Deciding If a Startup Accelerator Is Right for You 70
Conclusion 71

THANK YOU!!! 73

TAKE NOTES HERE 74

Chapter 1: Embracing the Frugal Mindset: The Lean Entrepreneur's Philosophy

Introduction

Welcome to "The Frugal Founder: Thriving in Entrepreneurship with Lean Principles"! As a budding entrepreneur, you may be brimming with innovative ideas and grand visions for your startup. However, navigating the world of entrepreneurship can be challenging, especially when faced with limited resources. The good news is, embracing a frugal mindset and following lean principles can set you on the path to success without breaking the bank. In this chapter, we'll explore the philosophy behind lean entrepreneurship and how adopting a frugal mindset can empower you to achieve more with less.

The Lean Entrepreneur's Philosophy

At the heart of lean entrepreneurship is the idea of doing more with less—achieving maximum value with minimal waste. By embracing a frugal mindset, you'll be able to focus on what truly matters, eliminating any unnecessary spending and finding creative solutions to challenges. Here are some key concepts that form the foundation of the lean entrepreneur's philosophy:

1. **Prioritize Value Creation**: Lean entrepreneurs focus on creating real value for their customers. This means understanding your target market's needs and desires and developing products or services that address them effectively. By prioritizing value creation, you'll develop a loyal customer base, which is crucial for long-term success.
2. **Emphasize Efficiency**: Efficiency is a cornerstone of the frugal mindset. It's about streamlining processes, reducing waste, and optimizing resource usage. Lean entrepreneurs constantly seek ways to improve their operations, often employing innovative solutions to boost productivity without incurring additional costs.
3. **Minimize Risk**: Startups, by their nature, involve risk. However, lean entrepreneurs strive to minimize risk by adopting a data-driven, iterative approach. This involves testing ideas and assumptions, gathering feedback, and making informed decisions based on evidence rather than relying solely on intuition.
4. **Adopt a Growth Mindset**: Lean entrepreneurs see challenges as opportunities for growth and learning. By cultivating a growth mindset, you'll be more open to exploring new ideas, adapting to change, and embracing failure as a valuable learning experience.
5. **Resourcefulness and Creativity**: Frugality doesn't mean compromising on quality.

Instead, it's about being resourceful and finding creative ways to achieve your goals with the resources at your disposal. This often involves thinking outside the box, identifying cost-effective solutions, and leveraging partnerships to maximize value.

How to Develop a Frugal Mindset

Now that you understand the core principles of the lean entrepreneur's philosophy, let's dive into some practical tips on how to develop a frugal mindset:

1. **Set Clear Goals and Priorities**: Begin by defining your startup's mission, vision, and goals. This will help you establish clear priorities and allocate resources more effectively. Remember to focus on activities that drive value creation and align with your long-term objectives.
2. **Track and Measure**: Keeping track of your expenses, revenue, and key performance indicators (KPIs) is essential for maintaining a frugal mindset. Regularly review your financials and analyze your data to identify areas for improvement and make informed decisions.
3. **Embrace Constraints**: Constraints can be a powerful catalyst for innovation. When faced with limited resources, challenge yourself to find creative ways to achieve your goals. This might involve rethinking your business model,

exploring alternative revenue streams, or forming strategic partnerships.
4. **Educate Yourself**: Continuously learning and expanding your knowledge will help you stay ahead of the curve and make smarter decisions. Attend workshops, read books, listen to podcasts, and network with other entrepreneurs to broaden your perspective and learn valuable lessons from their experiences.
5. **Practice Gratitude and Mindfulness**: Cultivating a positive mindset is crucial for maintaining your motivation and resilience as an entrepreneur. Practice gratitude by recognizing your achievements and appreciating the opportunities that come your way. Mindfulness can help you stay focused and present, enabling you to make more thoughtful decisions and maintain a healthy work-life balance.
6. **Challenge Assumptions**: Question your assumptions and challenge conventional wisdom. Just because something has always been done a certain way doesn't mean it's the most efficient or effective approach. Be open to experimentation and re-evaluating your strategies as needed.
7. **Stay Adaptable**: The world of entrepreneurship is constantly evolving, and staying adaptable is key to success. Be prepared to pivot your business model, adjust

your product or service offerings, and respond to market trends to stay competitive.

Frugal Mindset in Action: Real-Life Examples

To better understand the power of the frugal mindset, let's explore some real-life examples of successful entrepreneurs who have embraced lean principles:

1. **MailChimp**: The email marketing platform started as a side project for its founders, Ben Chestnut and Dan Kurzius. With a focus on simplicity and providing value to small businesses, MailChimp became profitable without the need for external funding. By bootstrapping their business and prioritizing customer needs, the founders built a company that now serves millions of users worldwide.
2. **Basecamp**: The popular project management tool was created by a small, remote team with limited resources. By focusing on building a simple, user-friendly product, Basecamp attracted a loyal customer base and generated steady revenue without relying on venture capital funding.
3. **Canva**: The graphic design platform was founded by Melanie Perkins, who started by bootstrapping the business and keeping costs low. Canva's success can be attributed to its focus on providing an easy-to-use tool for non-designers and constantly iterating on user feedback to improve the product.

By following the principles of lean entrepreneurship, these companies were able to achieve success without incurring significant debt or diluting ownership. Their stories demonstrate the power of embracing a frugal mindset and the value of resourcefulness, creativity, and efficiency.

Conclusion

As you embark on your entrepreneurial journey, remember that embracing a frugal mindset and adhering to lean principles can be the key to building a successful and sustainable business. By prioritizing value creation, focusing on efficiency, minimizing risk, and cultivating a growth mindset, you'll be well-positioned to navigate the challenges of entrepreneurship and make the most of your limited resources. Use the tips and real-life examples provided in this chapter as a starting point, and always stay open to learning, adapting, and growing. Best of luck on your exciting adventure!

Chapter 2: The Art of Bootstrapping: Funding Your Startup with Limited Resources

Introduction

So you've embraced the frugal mindset and are ready to dive into the world of entrepreneurship with your lean principles in hand. But how do you fund your startup with limited resources? The answer lies in bootstrapping – the process of building a business from scratch without relying on external funding. In this chapter, we'll explore the art of bootstrapping, providing you with practical tips and strategies to fund your startup and achieve success on a shoestring budget.

The Power of Bootstrapping

Bootstrapping offers several benefits for entrepreneurs, especially those who are just starting out. Some of the key advantages include:

1. **Maintaining Control**: When you bootstrap your business, you retain full ownership and control over your startup. This allows you to make decisions based on your vision and

priorities, without the pressure of pleasing investors or meeting external expectations.
2. **Cultivating Resourcefulness**: Bootstrapping forces you to be creative and resourceful in your approach to business. This mindset can help you uncover innovative solutions, streamline operations, and develop a more resilient and adaptable organization.
3. **Fostering Financial Discipline**: With limited funds, you'll need to carefully manage your expenses and prioritize investments that deliver the most value. This financial discipline will serve you well throughout your entrepreneurial journey.

Now that we've covered the benefits of bootstrapping, let's delve into some practical strategies for funding your startup with limited resources.

Bootstrapping Strategies for Success

1. **Start Small and Validate Your Idea**: Before investing significant time and resources into your startup, test and validate your business idea. Begin with a minimum viable product (MVP) – a simplified version of your product or service – and gather feedback from potential customers. This will help you refine your offering, identify your target market, and minimize the risk of failure.

2. **Keep Your Day Job**: While it may be tempting to dive headfirst into entrepreneurship, maintaining a steady source of income can provide you with the financial security you need to bootstrap your business. Use your spare time to work on your startup, and consider making the transition to full-time entrepreneurship once you've established a solid foundation.
3. **Leverage Your Personal Network**: Your friends, family, and professional contacts can be invaluable resources when bootstrapping your startup. Reach out for advice, introductions, or even small investments to help you get started. Remember to always be transparent about the risks involved and never pressure anyone into supporting your venture.
4. **Cut Costs and Operate Lean**: Reduce your expenses by operating as lean as possible. This may involve working from home, outsourcing tasks to freelancers, or utilizing free or low-cost tools and software. Keep track of your expenses and regularly evaluate where you can cut costs without sacrificing quality.
5. **Reinvest Profits**: As your startup begins to generate revenue, reinvest your profits into the business. This will help you grow and scale your operations without relying on external funding. Be strategic in your investments, prioritizing areas that will deliver the most value and drive growth.

6. **Explore Alternative Funding Options**: While bootstrapping is primarily about self-funding, there are alternative financing options available that may be suitable for your startup. These include grants, competitions, crowdfunding, or small business loans. Do your research and evaluate which options align best with your business goals and values.
7. **Network and Build Partnerships**: Building strong relationships and partnerships can be a powerful way to bootstrap your business. Attend networking events, join industry organizations, and engage with fellow entrepreneurs to expand your network. Form strategic partnerships with complementary businesses to share resources, expertise, and customer bases.

Conclusion

Bootstrapping may be challenging, but it can also be incredibly rewarding. By funding your startup with limited resources, you'll develop the resourcefulness, financial discipline, and resilience needed to succeed in the world of entrepreneurship. Remember that starting small, validating your idea, maintaining a steady income, leveraging your network, cutting costs, reinvesting profits, and exploring alternative funding options can all contribute to a successful bootstrapping journey.

As you embark on this path, stay focused on your vision and be prepared to adapt as you learn and grow. Embrace the challenges and celebrate your achievements, knowing that you are building a business that is truly your own. With dedication, hard work, and a little creativity, you'll be well on your way to becoming a successful, self-funded entrepreneur. Happy bootstrapping!

Chapter 3: Building a Lean Team: Hiring and Retaining Top Talent on a Budget

Introduction

As a frugal founder, you know the importance of operating with limited resources. One of the most critical aspects of building a successful startup is assembling a talented, dedicated team that shares your vision and passion. However, hiring and retaining top talent can be challenging, especially when you're working with a tight budget. In this chapter, we'll explore strategies for building a lean team that can help you grow and scale your business without breaking the bank.

The Importance of a Lean Team

A lean team is a small, efficient group of individuals who are committed to your startup's success. When building a lean team, it's essential to focus on quality over quantity. A small team of highly skilled, motivated individuals can often achieve more than a larger team with less focus and dedication. Some of the key advantages of a lean team include:

1. **Agility**: With a smaller team, decision-making and communication can be faster and more efficient, allowing your startup to pivot and adapt quickly as needed.

2. **Cost Savings**: A lean team helps you keep your expenses in check, enabling you to allocate resources to other critical aspects of your business.
3. **Stronger Relationships**: Building a close-knit team fosters trust, collaboration, and a sense of shared ownership in the startup's success.

Now that we've discussed the importance of a lean team let's delve into some practical strategies for hiring and retaining top talent on a budget.

Strategies for Building a Lean Team

1. **Define Your Core Team**: Before you start hiring, identify the critical roles and skillsets needed to drive your startup forward. Focus on filling these roles first, and be prepared to wear multiple hats as a founder until your business can support additional hires.
2. **Hire for Attitude and Potential**: While experience and skills are essential, finding candidates who share your passion and vision can be even more critical to your startup's success. Look for individuals who demonstrate a growth mindset, adaptability, and a strong work ethic. These traits often translate into high potential and can be more valuable than specific experience in the long run.
3. **Utilize Freelancers and Contractors**: Hiring freelancers or contractors can be a cost-effective way to access specialized skills on an

as-needed basis. This allows you to keep your core team lean while still benefiting from the expertise of professionals in various fields.
4. **Offer Non-Monetary Benefits**: While you may not be able to compete with larger companies in terms of salary, you can still attract top talent by offering unique non-monetary benefits. These might include flexible work arrangements, opportunities for professional development, or equity in the company.
5. **Create a Strong Company Culture**: A positive, inclusive, and supportive company culture can be a significant draw for talented professionals. Foster a work environment that encourages collaboration, open communication, and personal growth. This will not only help you attract top talent but also retain and motivate your team members.
6. **Leverage Your Network**: Tap into your personal and professional networks to find potential candidates for your team. Friends, former colleagues, and fellow entrepreneurs can be invaluable resources for recommendations and referrals. Additionally, consider attending industry events and networking functions to connect with potential hires.
7. **Develop an Employee Referral Program**: Encourage your current team members to refer qualified candidates for open positions. Offering incentives for successful referrals can

motivate your employees to actively participate in the hiring process and help you identify top talent that may not be found through traditional channels.

Retaining Top Talent on a Budget

Once you've assembled your lean team, it's essential to focus on retention. Here are some strategies to help you retain top talent without straining your budget:

1. **Recognize and Reward Success**: Show appreciation for your team's hard work and accomplishments through regular recognition and rewards. This could include verbal praise, written acknowledgment, or small gestures such as gift cards or team outings.
2. **Encourage Professional Growth**: Support your team members' professional development by offering opportunities for learning and growth. This might involve providing access to online courses, industry conferences, or mentorship programs.
3. **Foster Open Communication**: Create an environment where team members feel comfortable sharing their ideas, concerns, and feedback. Regular check-ins, team meetings, and an open-door policy can help facilitate open communication and ensure that everyone's voice is heard.

4. **Promote Work-Life Balance**: Encourage your team to maintain a healthy work-life balance by offering flexible work arrangements, setting realistic expectations, and respecting personal time.
5. **Provide Opportunities for Advancement**: As your startup grows, create clear paths for career progression within your organization. This will help your team members see a future with your company and feel motivated to contribute to its long-term success.

Conclusion

Building a lean team of top talent is a critical component of your startup's success. By focusing on hiring for attitude and potential, utilizing freelancers, offering non-monetary benefits, and fostering a strong company culture, you can attract and retain the right people even on a tight budget. Remember that nurturing your team, recognizing their achievements, and supporting their professional growth will help ensure their continued dedication and commitment to your startup's success. Good luck on your journey to building a lean, talented, and passionate team!

Chapter 4: Maximizing Minimum Viable Products: Testing and Validating Ideas with Less

Introduction

As a lean entrepreneur, one of your primary goals is to bring your product or service to market quickly while minimizing costs and risks. This is where the concept of the minimum viable product (MVP) comes into play. An MVP is a simplified version of your product that contains just enough features to satisfy early adopters and validate your business idea. In this chapter, we'll explore the process of creating, testing, and iterating on your MVP to maximize its potential and bring your vision to life.

The Power of Minimum Viable Products

An MVP offers several advantages for lean entrepreneurs, including:

1. **Speed to Market**: Creating an MVP allows you to launch your product or service quickly, capturing valuable feedback from early users and staying ahead of the competition.
2. **Cost Efficiency**: Developing an MVP requires fewer resources than a fully-featured product, reducing your initial investment and financial risk.

3. **Learning and Adaptation**: An MVP provides an opportunity to learn from real users, helping you identify and prioritize the most crucial features, improvements, and iterations for your product.
4. **Validation**: The MVP approach allows you to test your idea in the market, ensuring there's demand for your product before investing further time and resources.

With these benefits in mind, let's discuss how to maximize your MVP to test and validate your ideas with less.

Maximizing Your Minimum Viable Product

1. **Define Your Core Features**: Start by identifying the essential features and functionality that your MVP must include. Focus on what sets your product apart and solves a specific problem for your target audience. Remember, the goal is to provide just enough value to attract early adopters and gather feedback.
2. **Develop a Lean Prototype**: With your core features in mind, create a simplified prototype of your product. This can be a wireframe, mockup, or basic working model, depending on your product type. The purpose of the prototype is to test your assumptions, gather feedback, and refine your concept before moving on to the next stages of development.

3. **Test with Real Users**: Engage a small group of early adopters to test your MVP. These users should represent your target audience and be willing to provide honest feedback on their experience. Make it easy for them to share their thoughts, ask questions, and report any issues they encounter.
4. **Iterate and Improve**: Based on the feedback you receive, identify the areas where your MVP can be improved. Prioritize the most critical issues and enhancements, and make adjustments to your product accordingly. Remember, the goal is to learn and adapt quickly, so don't be afraid to make significant changes if necessary.
5. **Repeat the Process**: Continue testing and iterating on your MVP until you achieve a product-market fit – a point at which your product satisfies a strong market demand. This may require multiple iterations, so be prepared to remain flexible and responsive to user feedback.
6. **Scale and Expand**: Once you've validated your product and achieved product-market fit, you can begin to scale and expand your offerings. This may involve adding new features, targeting additional customer segments, or exploring new marketing channels. Be cautious not to overextend yourself; focus on sustainable growth and maintain your lean principles throughout the process.

Conclusion

Embracing the concept of the minimum viable product can be a game-changer for lean entrepreneurs. By focusing on core features, developing a lean prototype, testing with real users, and iterating quickly, you can validate your ideas, refine your product, and achieve success with fewer resources. Remember that the journey to product-market fit may be filled with challenges and surprises, but with dedication, persistence, and a focus on continuous improvement, you can maximize your MVP and bring your vision to life. Keep learning, adapting, and growing, and you'll be well on your way to creating a product that truly resonates with your target audience and delivers value to the market.

As you progress through this MVP journey, remember to stay true to your lean principles, prioritizing efficiency and resourcefulness at every step. The process may not always be smooth, but the lessons you learn and the insights you gain from your early adopters will be invaluable in shaping your product's future success.

By maximizing your minimum viable product, you can minimize risk and financial investment while maximizing learning and adaptability, ultimately creating a solid foundation for your startup's growth. So, embrace the power of the MVP, keep iterating, and stay focused on delivering value to your customers – your lean entrepreneurial journey has only just begun!

Chapter 5: Agile Marketing: Promoting Your Startup without Breaking the Bank

Introduction

Marketing your startup is crucial to its success, but as a lean entrepreneur, you may not have the budget for expensive campaigns or top-tier advertising agencies. Enter agile marketing – a flexible, data-driven approach to promoting your business that allows you to adapt quickly, make the most of your resources, and generate results without breaking the bank. In this chapter, we'll explore the principles of agile marketing and provide practical tips for promoting your startup on a budget.

Understanding Agile Marketing

Agile marketing is an iterative approach to marketing that focuses on flexibility, collaboration, and continuous improvement. It is inspired by the principles of agile software development and encourages marketers to:

1. Prioritize customer needs and preferences
2. Embrace experimentation and learning
3. Respond to change quickly and effectively
4. Measure results and make data-driven decisions
5. Collaborate and communicate openly

By adopting an agile marketing mindset, you can optimize your marketing efforts, maximize your budget, and drive growth for your startup.

Agile Marketing Strategies for Lean Entrepreneurs

1. **Set Clear Goals and Objectives**: Begin by defining your marketing goals and objectives. These should align with your overall business strategy and be specific, measurable, achievable, relevant, and time-bound (SMART).
2. **Develop a Marketing Plan**: Create a flexible marketing plan that outlines your target audience, key messages, channels, and tactics. Remember, the goal is to be agile and adaptable, so be prepared to revise your plan as you learn and gather data.
3. **Leverage Low-Cost Channels**: As a lean entrepreneur, focus on cost-effective marketing channels that offer a high return on investment (ROI). These might include social media, email marketing, content marketing, search engine optimization (SEO), and public relations (PR).
4. **Test and Experiment**: Use an iterative approach to test different marketing tactics, messages, and channels. Analyze your results, learn from your successes and failures, and adjust your strategy accordingly.
5. **Measure and Optimize**: Track your marketing efforts and measure their effectiveness using key performance indicators (KPIs). Use this data to optimize your campaigns, allocate resources,

and make informed decisions about your marketing strategy.
6. **Collaborate and Communicate**: Foster a culture of open communication and collaboration within your marketing team. Share insights, ideas, and feedback to improve your marketing efforts and drive results.

Practical Tips for Promoting Your Startup on a Budget

1. **Create Compelling Content**: Develop high-quality, engaging content that showcases your expertise, addresses your audience's pain points, and highlights the value of your product or service. Share this content on your website, blog, and social media platforms to attract and retain customers.
2. **Build a Strong Online Presence**: Optimize your website for search engines, create and maintain an active presence on relevant social media platforms, and leverage online communities and forums to engage with your target audience.
3. **Tap into Your Network**: Utilize your personal and professional networks to promote your startup. Ask friends, family, and colleagues to share your content, refer customers, or provide testimonials and reviews.
4. **Partner with Influencers**: Identify influencers within your industry who share your target audience and collaborate with them to

promote your product or service. This can involve sponsored content, product reviews, or co-created content.
5. **Leverage Email Marketing**: Build an email list and develop targeted email campaigns to nurture leads, engage customers, and promote your offerings. Email marketing is a cost-effective channel with a high ROI, making it ideal for lean entrepreneurs.
6. **Host Events and Webinars**: Organize online or in-person events and webinars to showcase your product, share your expertise, and connect with potential customers. This can help establish your brand as an industry authority while providing valuable networking opportunities.
7. **Utilize Public Relations (PR)**: Generate buzz for your startup through PR efforts. This can include pitching stories to journalists, submitting press releases, and engaging with industry influencers. A well executed PR campaign can help you gain valuable media coverage and credibility without a significant financial investment.
8. **Harness the Power of User-Generated Content (UGC)**: Encourage your customers to share their experiences with your product or service by creating and sharing user-generated content. This can include testimonials, reviews, social media posts, and more. UGC can be a

powerful, authentic, and cost-effective way to promote your startup.
9. **Engage in Social Listening**: Monitor social media and online discussions to understand what people are saying about your brand, industry, and competitors. Use these insights to inform your marketing strategy, identify potential opportunities, and address customer concerns.
10. **Refine and Iterate**: Continuously assess and adjust your marketing strategy based on the data you collect and the insights you gain. By staying agile and responsive, you can make the most of your limited resources and drive sustainable growth for your startup.

Conclusion

Agile marketing is an invaluable approach for lean entrepreneurs looking to promote their startups without breaking the bank. By embracing flexibility, experimentation, data-driven decision-making, and collaboration, you can optimize your marketing efforts and maximize your budget.

Remember to leverage low-cost channels, test and experiment with various tactics, and utilize your network to spread the word about your product or service. As you implement these strategies and refine your marketing plan, you'll be well on your way to achieving your goals and growing your startup in a sustainable, cost-effective manner.

Keep the agile marketing mindset at the core of your promotional efforts, and you'll be poised to adapt and thrive in the ever-changing world of entrepreneurship. Good luck, and happy marketing!

Chapter 6: Cost-Effective Customer Acquisition: Attracting and Retaining Clients the Lean Way

Introduction

As a lean entrepreneur, one of your primary objectives is to acquire and retain customers cost-effectively. This involves using creative, low-cost strategies to attract new clients and keep them coming back for more. In this chapter, we'll explore cost-effective customer acquisition techniques and best practices for retaining clients, all while staying true to your lean principles.

Cost-Effective Customer Acquisition Strategies

1. **Optimize Your Website**: Your website is often the first point of contact between your business and potential customers. Ensure that it is user-friendly, visually appealing, and optimized for search engines to increase visibility and drive organic traffic.
2. **Content Marketing**: Produce valuable, informative content that addresses your target audience's pain points and showcases your expertise. Share this content on your blog, social media platforms, and through email marketing to attract potential customers and establish your brand as an industry authority.

3. **Social Media Marketing**: Build a strong presence on relevant social media platforms to connect with your target audience and promote your brand. Share engaging content, participate in conversations, and leverage hashtags to increase your reach and visibility.
4. **Influencer Partnerships**: Collaborate with influencers in your industry to tap into their audience and build credibility for your brand. This could involve sponsored posts, product reviews, or co-created content.
5. **Referral Programs**: Encourage satisfied customers to refer friends, family, or colleagues to your business by offering incentives, such as discounts or rewards. Referral programs can be a cost-effective way to acquire new customers through word-of-mouth marketing.
6. **Network and Build Relationships**: Attend industry events, conferences, and networking functions to connect with potential customers, partners, and influencers. Building strong relationships can lead to new business opportunities and increased brand awareness.
7. **Leverage Free or Low-Cost Tools**: Utilize free or low-cost marketing tools, such as email marketing platforms, social media management tools, and analytics software, to streamline and optimize your customer acquisition efforts.

Retaining Clients the Lean Way

1. **Deliver Exceptional Customer Service**: Providing outstanding customer service is crucial for retaining clients and building long-term relationships. Respond to inquiries promptly, address concerns effectively, and go the extra mile to exceed customer expectations.
2. **Personalize the Customer Experience**: Tailor your communication and marketing efforts to individual customer preferences, needs, and interests. Personalization can help create a strong connection between your brand and your clients, increasing customer satisfaction and loyalty.
3. **Offer Incentives for Repeat Business**: Encourage repeat business by offering discounts, loyalty programs, or exclusive offers for returning customers. These incentives can help foster customer loyalty and increase your customer lifetime value.
4. **Seek and Implement Feedback**: Regularly solicit feedback from your clients to identify areas for improvement and implement changes based on their suggestions. Demonstrating that you value their opinions and are committed to continuous improvement can help build trust and loyalty.
5. **Stay Engaged with Your Customers**: Maintain an ongoing dialogue with your clients through email, social media, or other communication

channels. Share updates, news, and helpful tips to keep your brand top-of-mind and demonstrate your ongoing commitment to their success.
6. **Continuously Innovate and Improve**: Stay ahead of your competition and anticipate your customers' evolving needs by continuously updating and improving your product or service offerings.

Conclusion

Attracting and retaining clients the lean way is all about being resourceful, adaptable, and customer-focused. By implementing cost-effective customer acquisition strategies and prioritizing customer satisfaction and retention, you can grow your business while staying true to your lean principles.

Remember that the key to success in customer acquisition and retention is to stay agile, learn from your experiences, and continually refine your approach based on data and feedback. Keep your customers at the heart of everything you do, and you'll be well on your way to building a loyal client base that drives sustainable growth for your startup.

As you embark on this journey, stay focused on delivering value, exceeding expectations, and fostering long-term relationships with your clients. By doing so, you'll not only attract new customers but also turn them into brand advocates who will spread the word about your business and help fuel your success.

In summary, remember to:

1. Optimize your website for search engines and user experience
2. Create valuable content that addresses your audience's needs
3. Leverage social media and influencer partnerships
4. Encourage referrals and word-of-mouth marketing
5. Network and build strong relationships within your industry
6. Deliver exceptional customer service and personalized experiences
7. Continuously seek feedback and innovate to stay ahead of the competition

By implementing these strategies and embracing the lean way of acquiring and retaining customers, you'll be well-positioned to grow your startup in a cost-effective and sustainable manner. Good luck, and happy customer hunting!

Chapter 7: Streamlining Operations: How to Eliminate Waste and Boost Efficiency

Introduction

Efficient operations are the backbone of any successful lean startup. By streamlining your processes, eliminating waste, and continuously improving your systems, you can drive productivity, reduce costs, and create a more sustainable business model. In this chapter, we'll explore practical strategies for streamlining your operations and boosting efficiency, all while staying true to your lean entrepreneurial principles.

Identifying Waste in Your Operations

Before you can eliminate waste, you need to identify areas of inefficiency within your operations. Waste can take many forms, including:

1. **Overproduction**: Producing more goods or services than needed, leading to excess inventory and storage costs.
2. **Waiting**: Delays in processes, such as waiting for materials, approvals, or information.
3. **Transportation**: Unnecessary movement of materials, products, or information between processes.

4. **Overprocessing**: Performing more work than necessary or using overly complex solutions.
5. **Inventory**: Excess stock or materials that incur storage costs and tie up capital.
6. **Motion**: Unnecessary movement of people, such as searching for tools or equipment.
7. **Defects**: Errors or defects in products or services that require rework, repairs, or replacements.

By analyzing your operations and identifying areas of waste, you can develop targeted strategies for improvement and create a more efficient, cost-effective business.

Strategies for Streamlining Operations

1. **Map Your Processes**: Create a visual representation of your current processes, highlighting each step, decision point, and potential bottleneck. This will help you identify areas of waste, inefficiency, and duplication.
2. **Standardize and Simplify**: Establish standard operating procedures (SOPs) for each process, ensuring that tasks are performed consistently and efficiently. Simplify your processes by eliminating unnecessary steps or combining tasks where possible.
3. **Implement Continuous Improvement**: Encourage a culture of continuous improvement within your organization by regularly reviewing and refining your

processes. Utilize feedback from your team, customers, and suppliers to identify areas for improvement and implement changes accordingly.
4. **Automate and Delegate**: Leverage technology to automate repetitive tasks and streamline your operations. Delegate tasks to your team members, ensuring that each person is working on tasks that align with their skills and expertise.
5. **Optimize Your Workspace**: Organize your physical workspace to minimize motion waste and improve efficiency. Implement the 5S methodology (Sort, Set in Order, Shine, Standardize, and Sustain) to create an organized, clutter-free environment that supports productivity.
6. **Embrace Just-In-Time (JIT) Inventory Management**: Reduce inventory waste by implementing a JIT inventory system, which involves ordering materials and supplies as needed, rather than maintaining large stockpiles. This can help you minimize storage costs, reduce the risk of obsolescence, and improve cash flow.
7. **Measure and Monitor**: Track key performance indicators (KPIs) to assess the efficiency of your operations and identify areas for improvement. Regularly review your performance data and adjust your processes and strategies as needed.

Boosting Efficiency through Lean Principles

As a lean entrepreneur, you can apply the following lean principles to further streamline your operations and boost efficiency:

1. **Value**: Understand and prioritize the needs of your customers, focusing on delivering value at every stage of your operations.
2. **Value Stream**: Identify and optimize the flow of value through your processes, eliminating waste and ensuring that each step contributes to customer satisfaction.
3. **Flow**: Establish smooth, uninterrupted workflows within your organization, reducing delays and minimizing waiting time.
4. **Pull**: Create a demand-driven system that produces goods or services only when required, minimizing overproduction and inventory waste.
5. **Perfection**: Continuously strive for perfection in your operations, seeking opportunities for improvement and learning from mistakes and successes.
6. **Empower Your Team**: Involve your team members in the process of identifying waste and improving operations. Encourage open communication, creative problem-solving, and a sense of ownership over the success of your business.

7. **Build a Culture of Learning**: Foster a learning environment where team members can continually develop their skills, stay current with industry trends, and contribute to the ongoing improvement of your operations.

Conclusion

Streamlining your operations and boosting efficiency are critical components of a successful lean startup. By identifying and eliminating waste, implementing continuous improvement, and applying lean principles, you can create a more agile, cost-effective, and sustainable business model.

Remember that the journey towards operational excellence is an ongoing process that requires commitment, adaptability, and a focus on delivering value to your customers. As you implement these strategies and refine your operations, you'll be well on your way to achieving your goals and growing your startup in a lean, efficient manner.

Stay focused on the principles of lean entrepreneurship, and you'll be well-positioned to navigate the challenges and opportunities that come your way. Good luck, and happy streamlining!

Chapter 8: Scaling Smart: Growing Your Business with Lean Principles

Introduction

Scaling your business is an exciting and challenging phase for any entrepreneur, especially for those committed to the lean methodology. Growing your business with lean principles means making strategic decisions, prioritizing efficiency, and maintaining a focus on delivering value to your customers. In this chapter, we'll explore how to scale your business smartly while staying true to your lean entrepreneurial values.

Key Factors for Smart Scaling

1. **Validate Your Market**: Before investing time, effort, and resources into scaling your business, it's crucial to validate that there's a growing market for your product or service. Conduct market research, analyze industry trends, and gather feedback from your customers to ensure that there's a strong demand for what you're offering.

2. **Focus on Your Core Competencies**: As you grow your business, it's essential to maintain a clear focus on your core competencies. Identify what you do best and what differentiates you from your competitors. Then, allocate your resources and efforts to improve and expand

these areas, ensuring that your business stays competitive and relevant.
3. **Optimize Your Processes**: Scaling smartly means maximizing efficiency in your operations. Continuously review and refine your processes, eliminate waste, and streamline your workflows to boost productivity and reduce costs.
4. **Build a Strong Team**: As your business grows, you'll need a talented and committed team to support your vision. Hire individuals who align with your company culture and values, and invest in their professional development. Empower your team members by delegating tasks, fostering open communication, and encouraging collaboration.
5. **Prioritize Customer Success**: Maintaining a strong focus on customer success is vital as you scale your business. Continuously improve your products and services, offer exceptional customer support, and prioritize customer satisfaction. Building strong relationships with your customers will not only help you retain them but also turn them into brand advocates who can spread the word about your business.

Strategies for Scaling with Lean Principles

1. **Lean Startup Methodology**: Embrace the Lean Startup methodology by continuously testing and validating your assumptions, iterating on your products and services, and learning from

both successes and failures. This approach will help you make informed decisions, minimize risks, and ensure that your business stays agile as it grows.
2. **Build a Scalable Business Model**: Develop a business model that can accommodate growth without significant increases in costs or complexity. This may involve leveraging technology, automating processes, or outsourcing non-core functions.
3. **Experiment with Growth Strategies**: Test different growth strategies, such as expanding to new markets, diversifying your product offerings, or forming strategic partnerships. Continuously assess the effectiveness of these strategies and refine your approach based on data and insights.
4. **Measure and Monitor**: Track key performance indicators (KPIs) to gauge the success of your scaling efforts and identify areas for improvement. Regularly review your performance data and adjust your strategies as needed to ensure that you're making progress towards your goals.
5. **Maintain Financial Discipline**: As you scale your business, it's essential to maintain financial discipline and control your costs. Continuously monitor your expenses, optimize your cash flow, and prioritize investments that deliver the greatest value and return.

6. **Embrace a Culture of Continuous Improvement**: Foster a culture of continuous improvement within your organization, encouraging your team to identify opportunities for growth and efficiency. Implement changes based on feedback and lessons learned, and continuously strive to improve your products, services, and operations.

Conclusion

Scaling your business with lean principles is all about making strategic, data-driven decisions that prioritize efficiency, customer success, and long-term sustainability. By focusing on your core competencies, optimizing your processes, and building a strong team, you can grow your business smartly and effectively.

Remember that scaling smartly requires an ongoing commitment to learning, adapting, and refining your approach based on feedback and data. As you navigate the challenges and opportunities of growth, stay true to your lean entrepreneurial values and maintain a focus on delivering value to your customers.

In summary, when scaling your business with lean principles, be sure to:

1. Validate your market and focus on your core competencies.
2. Optimize your processes and build a strong team.
3. Prioritize customer success and maintain financial discipline.
4. Embrace the Lean Startup methodology and build a scalable business model.
5. Experiment with growth strategies and continuously improve.

By implementing these strategies and embracing a growth mindset, you'll be well-positioned to scale your business successfully while staying true to your lean principles. Good luck, and happy scaling!

Chapter 9: Partnerships and Collaborations: Leveraging Networks for Mutual Success

Introduction

As a lean entrepreneur, forging strategic partnerships and collaborations can be an effective way to grow your business, expand your reach, and access valuable resources without incurring significant costs. By leveraging networks and joining forces with like-minded individuals or organizations, you can create mutually beneficial relationships that drive success for all parties involved. In this chapter, we'll explore the benefits of partnerships and collaborations and provide practical tips for building strong, lasting relationships that support your lean startup's growth.

The Benefits of Partnerships and Collaborations

1. **Access to New Markets**: Collaborating with partners who have established networks and customer bases can help you tap into new markets and expand your reach more quickly and cost-effectively than if you were to go it alone.
2. **Shared Resources**: Partnerships can provide access to valuable resources, such as technology, expertise, or facilities, that might otherwise be too expensive or time-consuming to acquire independently.
3. **Cost Savings**: By pooling resources and sharing costs, partnerships can help reduce expenses, allowing you to invest in other areas of your business.

4. **Innovation**: Collaborations can lead to the cross-pollination of ideas and the development of innovative products or services that may not have been possible without the combined expertise and perspectives of different partners.
5. **Credibility**: Aligning with established, reputable partners can lend credibility to your startup, helping you build trust with potential customers, investors, and suppliers.

Strategies for Building Successful Partnerships and Collaborations

1. **Define Clear Objectives**: Before entering into a partnership or collaboration, it's important to establish clear objectives and expectations for both parties. Understand what each party hopes to achieve from the relationship and ensure that these goals are aligned.
2. **Identify Complementary Partners**: Seek partners who have complementary skills, resources, and networks that can help fill gaps in your own business. By working with partners who bring different strengths to the table, you can create more value together than you could individually.
3. **Establish Open Communication**: Effective communication is essential for a successful partnership. Keep lines of communication open, transparent, and honest, and encourage regular check-ins to discuss progress, challenges, and opportunities.
4. **Foster Trust and Mutual Respect**: Building trust and respect between partners takes time and effort. Be reliable, honor your commitments, and be willing to listen and learn from your partner. By demonstrating your commitment to the partnership,

you'll be more likely to build a strong, lasting relationship.
5. **Share Risks and Rewards**: Ensure that both parties have a stake in the partnership's success by sharing risks and rewards fairly. Develop a mutually beneficial agreement that outlines each party's contributions, responsibilities, and benefits.
6. **Continuously Evaluate and Adjust**: As with any aspect of your business, it's important to regularly evaluate the success of your partnerships and collaborations. Assess whether your objectives are being met, and be open to adjusting your approach or redefining your goals as needed.

Tips for Nurturing and Maintaining Partnerships

1. **Celebrate Success**: Recognize and celebrate your partnership's successes, no matter how small. This will help reinforce the value of the relationship and motivate both parties to continue working together effectively.
2. **Address Challenges Proactively**: Inevitably, challenges will arise in any partnership. Address these issues proactively, and work together to find solutions that benefit both parties.
3. **Invest in the Relationship**: Building strong partnerships takes time and effort. Be willing to invest in the relationship, both personally and professionally, by attending events, participating in meetings, and staying engaged with your partner's activities.
4. **Be Adaptable**: As your business grows and evolves, your partnerships may need to evolve as well. Be open to change and adaptable to new circumstances, ensuring that your partnerships remain aligned with your current goals and needs.

5. **Maintain a Long-Term Perspective**: Approach partnerships with a long-term perspective, recognizing that the greatest benefits may not be immediately apparent. By focusing on the big picture and nurturing your relationships over time, you'll be better positioned to reap the rewards of your collaborative efforts.

Conclusion

Partnerships and collaborations can be powerful tools for lean entrepreneurs seeking to grow their businesses and achieve mutual success. By identifying complementary partners, establishing clear objectives, and fostering trust and open communication, you can build strong, lasting relationships that benefit all parties involved.

Remember that nurturing and maintaining partnerships takes time, effort, and a commitment to continuous improvement. By investing in your relationships and adapting your approach as needed, you'll be well-positioned to leverage networks and collaborations for the long-term success of your lean startup.

In summary, when forming partnerships and collaborations:

1. Define clear objectives and identify complementary partners.
2. Establish open communication and foster trust and mutual respect.
3. Share risks and rewards fairly, and continuously evaluate and adjust your approach.
4. Celebrate success, address challenges proactively, and invest in the relationship.

5. Maintain a long-term perspective and be adaptable to change.

By embracing these strategies, you'll be well on your way to building successful partnerships that support your lean startup's growth and help you achieve your entrepreneurial goals. Good luck, and happy collaborating!

Chapter 10: The Frugal Founder's Toolkit: Essential Resources and Strategies for Lean Entrepreneurship

Introduction

As a lean entrepreneur, having access to the right tools, resources, and strategies is crucial for managing your business effectively and efficiently. In this chapter, we'll explore the essential elements of a frugal founder's toolkit, covering everything from productivity tools and marketing resources to strategies for managing your time and finances.

Productivity and Organization Tools

1. **Project Management**: Tools like Trello, Asana, and Basecamp can help you manage tasks, deadlines, and team collaboration, ensuring that your projects stay on track and organized.
2. **Time Tracking**: Apps like Toggle, Harvest, and Clockify can help you track your time, analyze your productivity, and optimize your work habits.
3. **Note-taking and Document Collaboration**: Tools like Evernote, Google Docs, and Microsoft OneNote can help you capture ideas, collaborate on documents, and keep your files organized and accessible from anywhere.
4. **Communication and Collaboration**: Platforms like Slack, Microsoft Teams, and Zoom can help you communicate effectively with your team, schedule meetings, and host video conferences.
5. **Automation and Integration**: Tools like Zapier and IFTTT can help you automate repetitive tasks

and streamline your workflows by connecting your favorite apps and services.

Marketing Resources

1. **Social Media Management**: Tools like Buffer, Hootsuite, and Sprout Social can help you schedule, manage, and analyze your social media posts across multiple platforms.
2. **Email Marketing**: Platforms like Mailchimp, SendinBlue, and ConvertKit can help you create, send, and track email campaigns to engage your audience and grow your subscriber list.
3. **Content Creation**: Tools like Canva, Adobe Spark, and Pablo can help you create eye-catching visuals and graphics for your marketing materials, social media posts, and website.
4. **Analytics**: Google Analytics and other web analytics tools can help you track your website traffic, measure the performance of your marketing campaigns, and make data-driven decisions to optimize your marketing efforts.
5. **SEO**: Tools like Moz, Ahrefs, and SEMrush can help you analyze your website's search engine optimization (SEO), identify opportunities for improvement, and track your progress.

Financial Management

1. **Budgeting and Expense Tracking**: Tools like Mint, YNAB, and Expensify can help you create budgets, track expenses, and manage your personal and business finances.
2. **Invoicing and Payments**: Platforms like FreshBooks, QuickBooks, and Wave can help you create professional invoices, manage your clients, and accept payments online.
3. **Financial Planning and Analysis**: Spreadsheets like Microsoft Excel or Google Sheets can help you

create financial projections, analyze your cash flow, and evaluate your business's financial health.

Time Management and Self-Care

1. **Prioritize Tasks**: Use the Eisenhower Matrix or the ABCDE method to prioritize tasks based on their urgency and importance.
2. **Set SMART Goals**: Establish **S**pecific, **M**easurable, **A**chievable, **R**elevant, and **T**ime-bound goals to guide your actions and help you stay focused on your objectives.
3. **Break Tasks into Manageable Chunks**: Use the Pomodoro Technique or other time management methods to break your work into focused intervals, with short breaks in between.
4. **Maintain Work-Life Balance**: Schedule time for self-care, exercise, and relaxation to ensure you stay mentally and physically healthy, and avoid burnout.
5. **Continuous Learning**: Invest in your personal and professional development by reading books, attending workshops, or participating in online courses related to your industry or areas of interest.

Conclusion

Building your frugal founder's toolkit is an essential step in establishing a lean and efficient entrepreneurial journey. By leveraging the right tools, resources, and strategies, you can manage your business effectively, make informed decisions, and stay focused on your goals. Remember that the most important aspect of lean entrepreneurship is continuous improvement, so be open to exploring new tools and refining your processes as your business grows and evolves.

In summary, when building your frugal founder's toolkit:

1. Choose productivity and organization tools that fit your needs and help streamline your workflows.
2. Utilize marketing resources to create engaging content, manage your social media presence, and analyze your campaigns' performance.
3. Adopt financial management tools to track expenses, create invoices, and analyze your business's financial health.
4. Implement effective time management and self-care strategies to stay focused, maintain work-life balance, and avoid burnout.
5. Embrace continuous learning and invest in your personal and professional development.

By incorporating these essential resources and strategies into your daily routine, you'll be well-equipped to navigate the challenges of lean entrepreneurship and build a successful, sustainable business. Good luck, and happy frugal founding!

Bonus Chapter: Getting Featured in News by Journalists and Contributors

Introduction

As a lean entrepreneur, one of your main goals is to spread the word about your startup without breaking the bank. A powerful way to achieve this is by getting featured in news stories, articles, and interviews, which can provide valuable exposure, build credibility, and attract potential customers, investors, and partners. In this bonus chapter, we'll guide you through the process of connecting with journalists and contributors to share your story and get your startup the attention it deserves.

Why Getting Featured in News Matters

1. **Increased Visibility**: Being featured in news stories and articles can significantly increase your startup's visibility and reach, helping you attract new customers, investors, and partners.
2. **Enhanced Credibility**: When your startup is covered by reputable media outlets, it lends credibility to your business, making it easier to build trust with your target audience.
3. **Cost-Effective Marketing**: Unlike paid advertising, getting featured in news stories is usually free, making it an incredibly cost-effective way to promote your startup.

4. **Networking Opportunities**: Connecting with journalists and contributors can help you build valuable relationships with key influencers in your industry, opening doors to new opportunities and collaborations.

Strategies for Getting Featured in News

1. **Craft a Compelling Story**: To capture the attention of journalists and contributors, you need to present your startup in a way that's interesting, unique, and relevant. Develop a compelling narrative that highlights your startup's mission, impact, and accomplishments, and be prepared to share this story in a concise and engaging manner.
2. **Research and Target Relevant Media Outlets**: Identify the media outlets and journalists that cover topics related to your industry or niche. Create a list of potential targets, including local, national, and international publications, blogs, podcasts, and social media influencers.
3. **Build Relationships with Journalists and Contributors**: Start engaging with your target journalists and contributors by following them on social media, commenting on their articles, and sharing their content. This will help you establish a connection and demonstrate your interest in their work before reaching out with a pitch.

4. **Pitch Your Story**: Craft a personalized, well-researched pitch that clearly explains the value of your story and why it's relevant to the journalist's audience. Keep your pitch concise and focused, and be prepared to provide additional information or materials upon request.
5. **Be Responsive and Accommodating**: If a journalist or contributor expresses interest in your story, be sure to respond promptly and professionally. Provide any requested information or resources, and be flexible when it comes to scheduling interviews or answering follow-up questions.
6. **Leverage Your Network**: Tap into your personal and professional network to identify connections who may have relationships with journalists or contributors. Ask for introductions or recommendations to help you gain credibility and increase your chances of getting featured.
7. **Monitor and Leverage Media Opportunities**: Regularly monitor platforms like Help a Reporter Out (HARO), ProfNet, or JournoRequests for relevant media opportunities, and be prepared to respond quickly with a compelling pitch.

Maximizing the Impact of Your Media Coverage

1. **Share and Promote**: Once your startup is featured in a news story or article, share it

across your social media channels, website, and email newsletter. Encourage your team, friends, and family to share the coverage as well to increase its reach and impact.
2. **Create a Media Kit**: Compile all your media coverage in a media kit that can be easily accessed from your website. This will serve as a resource for potential customers, investors, and partners who want to learn more about your startup and its accomplishments.
3. **Leverage the Coverage in Your Marketing Materials**: Include logos, quotes, or snippets from your media coverage in your marketing materials, such as brochures, presentations, and website. This will help to enhance your credibility and showcase your startup's success.
4. **Follow Up and Maintain Relationships**: After your coverage is published, thank the journalist or contributor and maintain your relationship with them. Stay in touch, share relevant updates about your startup, and be open to future collaboration. This will increase your chances of being featured again in the future.
5. **Track and Measure the Impact**: Use analytics tools like Google Analytics to track the impact of your media coverage on your website traffic, social media engagement, and other key performance indicators (KPIs). This will help you understand the effectiveness of your efforts and identify areas for improvement.

Conclusion

Getting featured in news stories by journalists and contributors can be a game-changer for your lean startup, providing valuable exposure, credibility, and networking opportunities at minimal cost. By crafting a compelling story, targeting relevant media outlets, and building relationships with journalists and contributors, you can increase your chances of getting your startup the attention it deserves.

Remember to leverage your media coverage in your marketing materials, maintain relationships with journalists and contributors, and continually monitor and respond to media opportunities. By embracing these strategies and staying persistent, you'll be well on your way to becoming a news-worthy success story in the world of lean entrepreneurship. Good luck, and happy pitching!

Bonus Chapter: How to Find the Right Co-founder

Introduction

Finding the right co-founder is a critical decision for any entrepreneur, especially when building a lean startup. A great co-founder can bring complementary skills, experience, and connections to the table, while also providing invaluable support, motivation, and guidance throughout your entrepreneurial journey. In this bonus chapter, we'll explore the steps and strategies for finding the perfect co-founder to help you build a successful, sustainable business.

The Importance of a Co-founder

1. **Shared Workload**: A co-founder can help share the workload and responsibilities, allowing you to focus on your areas of expertise and ensuring that your startup runs more efficiently.
2. **Complementary Skills**: The right co-founder can bring unique skills and experiences that complement your own, enabling your startup to benefit from a broader range of expertise.
3. **Emotional Support**: Building a startup can be an emotional rollercoaster, and having a co-

founder can provide much-needed support, encouragement, and motivation during challenging times.
4. **Decision-Making**: A co-founder can offer fresh perspectives and insights, helping you make more informed decisions and avoid potential pitfalls.
5. **Networking Opportunities**: A co-founder with an extensive network can help you access new customers, partners, and investors, opening doors to new opportunities and growth.

Finding the Right Co-founder

1. **Identify Your Needs**: Start by assessing your own skills, strengths, and weaknesses, and identify the areas where you need support or complementary expertise. This will help you understand the qualities and skills you should be looking for in a co-founder.
2. **Expand Your Network**: Attend industry events, conferences, and meetups, and join online forums and communities related to your niche. These networking opportunities can help you connect with like-minded individuals who may be potential co-founders.
3. **Leverage Existing Relationships**: Consider reaching out to friends, colleagues, or acquaintances who may be interested in joining your startup as a co-founder. These individuals may already have a solid understanding of your work ethic, goals, and

vision, making the collaboration more seamless.
4. **Use Co-founder Matching Platforms**: Websites and platforms like CoFoundersLab, Founder2be, and Startup Weekend can help you connect with potential co-founders by allowing you to create a profile, search for candidates, and engage in conversations with like-minded individuals.
5. **Assess Cultural Fit**: In addition to evaluating potential co-founders based on their skills and experience, consider their cultural fit with your startup. Look for individuals who share your values, work ethic, and vision for the future.
6. **Test the Partnership**: Before making a formal commitment, consider working together on a small project or task to gauge your compatibility, communication, and ability to collaborate effectively.

Formalizing the Co-founder Relationship

1. **Define Roles and Responsibilities**: Clearly outline each co-founder's roles and responsibilities, ensuring that both parties understand their respective duties and expectations.
2. **Establish Ownership and Equity**: Discuss and agree upon ownership percentages, vesting schedules, and any other equity-related details to prevent potential disputes down the line.

3. **Create a Founders' Agreement**: Formalize your co-founder relationship with a written agreement that outlines roles, responsibilities, equity, decision-making processes, and any other relevant terms and conditions.
4. **Plan for Conflict Resolution**: Establish a process for resolving conflicts and disagreements to ensure that your co-founder relationship remains healthy and productive.
5. **Stay Open to Feedback and Adaptation**: Maintain open communication, be receptive to feedback, and be willing to adapt your roles and responsibilities as your startup grows and evolves.

Conclusion

Finding the right co-founder is an essential step in building a successful lean startup. By identifying your needs, expanding your network, and carefully evaluating potential candidates, you can find a co-founder who shares your vision, complements your skills, and provides the support and expertise necessary to help your business thrive. Remember to formalize your co-founder relationship with a clear agreement, establish processes for conflict resolution, and maintain open communication to foster a healthy, productive partnership.

As you embark on this journey, keep in mind that finding the right co-founder may take time and effort, but the rewards of a strong partnership will be well worth the investment. With the right co-founder by your side, you'll be better equipped to navigate the challenges of lean entrepreneurship and build a successful, sustainable business together. Good luck, and happy co-founder hunting!

Bonus Chapter: Should I Bother Participating in a Startup Accelerator?

Introduction

As a lean entrepreneur, you may be wondering if participating in a startup accelerator is worth the time and effort. Startup accelerators can provide valuable resources, mentorship, and networking opportunities, but they also require commitment and dedication. In this bonus chapter, we'll explore the benefits and drawbacks of joining a startup accelerator and help you determine if this path is the right fit for your lean startup.

Understanding Startup Accelerators

Startup accelerators are intensive, short-term programs designed to help early-stage startups scale quickly and efficiently. These programs typically last between three and six months and offer a combination of mentorship, resources, office space, and funding in exchange for a small percentage of equity in your startup. Some well-known startup accelerators include Y Combinator, Techstars, and 500 Startups.

The Pros of Joining a Startup Accelerator

1. **Access to Funding**: Many accelerators provide startups with seed funding, typically in exchange for a small percentage of equity. This funding can help you cover essential expenses and accelerate your growth without incurring significant debt.
2. **Mentorship and Expertise**: Accelerators often connect startups with experienced mentors, industry experts, and successful entrepreneurs who can provide invaluable guidance and insights as you navigate the challenges of building your business.
3. **Networking Opportunities**: Participating in a startup accelerator can help you build connections with other entrepreneurs, investors, and potential partners, opening doors to new opportunities and collaborations.
4. **Structured Curriculum**: Accelerators typically offer a structured curriculum that covers topics such as business strategy, product development, marketing, and fundraising. This curriculum can help you refine your business model, develop new skills, and avoid common pitfalls.
5. **Increased Credibility**: Being accepted into a prestigious accelerator program can enhance your startup's credibility, making it easier to attract customers, investors, and partners.

The Cons of Joining a Startup Accelerator

1. **Equity Stake**: In exchange for the resources and support provided by the accelerator, you'll often be required to give up a small percentage of your startup's equity. This may be a drawback for entrepreneurs who are hesitant to relinquish ownership or control of their business.
2. **Time Commitment**: Participating in an accelerator program can be time-consuming and may require you to temporarily relocate or dedicate a significant portion of your time to the program. This can be challenging for entrepreneurs with limited time or competing priorities.
3. **Limited Flexibility**: Accelerators often have strict schedules and deadlines, which may limit your flexibility and ability to pursue alternative growth strategies or pivot your business model.
4. **Competition for Acceptance**: Gaining entry into a prestigious accelerator program can be highly competitive, and the application process can be time-consuming and resource-intensive.

Deciding If a Startup Accelerator Is Right for You

To determine if joining a startup accelerator is the right choice for your lean startup, consider the following questions:

1. Are you willing to give up equity in exchange for the resources and support provided by the accelerator?
2. Can you commit the time and effort required to participate fully in the program?
3. Do you believe that the mentorship, resources, and networking opportunities offered by the accelerator will significantly impact your startup's growth and success?
4. Are you prepared to adhere to a structured curriculum and potentially pivot your business model based on the guidance and feedback received during the program?

If your answer to these questions is "yes," then participating in a startup accelerator may be a valuable opportunity for your lean startup. However, if you're hesitant about any of these factors, it may be worth exploring alternative strategies for growth and support.

Conclusion

Participating in a startup accelerator can be a transformative experience for lean entrepreneurs, offering access to funding, mentorship, and networking opportunities that can help your startup grow and thrive. However, it's essential to weigh the benefits and drawbacks of joining an accelerator program and carefully consider whether it aligns with your startup's needs, goals, and priorities.

If you decide that joining an accelerator is the right choice for your lean startup, take the time to research various programs and select the one that best aligns with your vision, values, and industry focus. And remember, while accelerators can provide valuable resources and support, the ultimate success of your startup depends on your hard work, dedication, and ability to adapt and innovate.

On the other hand, if you determine that an accelerator program isn't the right fit for your lean startup, don't be discouraged. There are many other avenues for growth and support, such as mentorship programs, online resources, and industry-specific communities. By staying focused on your goals and leveraging available resources, you can build a successful, sustainable business without participating in a startup accelerator.

Thank you!!!

Hope my tips and suggestions from my personal entrepreneurship journey have helped you in your journey. I often post entrepreneurship related contents on my social media channels as follows:

LinkedIn: http://linkedin.com/in/somdipdey
Facebook: http://facebook.com/deysomdip
Koo: http://kooapp.com/profile/somdipdey

Let's stay in touch and help each other to build businesses that matters!

Take Notes Here